Can't Stop Rhymin' on the Range

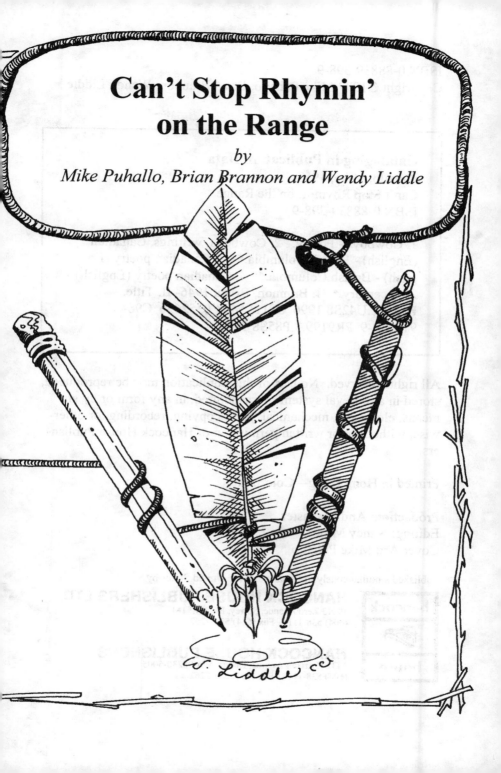

Can't Stop Rhymin' on the Range

by
Mike Puhallo, Brian Brannon and Wendy Liddle

ISBN 0-88839-398-9

Cataloging in Publication Data
Puhallo, Mike, 1953-
Can't Stop Rhymin' on the Range
ISBN 0-88839-398-9

1. Cowboys - Poetry.   2. Cowboys' writings, Canadian
(English) - British Columbia.*   3. Canadian poetry (En-
glish) - British Columbia.*   4. Canadian poetry (English) -
20th century.*   I. Brannon, Brian, 1946- II. Title.
PS8581.U42S8 1996 C811'.5408'0352636 C96-
910029-9 PR9199.3.P85S8 1996

Printed in Hong Kong—Colorcraft

Production: Andrew Jaster
Editing: Nancy Miller
Cover Art: Mike Puhallo

Published simultaneously in Canada and the United States by

HANCOCK HOUSE PUBLISHERS LTD.
19313 Zero Avenue, Surrey, BC V4P 1M7
(604) 538-1114   Fax (604) 538-2262

HANCOCK HOUSE PUBLISHERS
1431 Harrison Avenue, Blaine, WA 98230-5005
(604) 538-1114   Fax (604) 538-2262

Contents

W. Liddle, cci

Dedication

This, the third book in what has become a trilogy, is dedicated to those people who still have a wiff of campfire smoke in their nostrils. It is your patronage which has made this and the two previous books a viable exercise for all concerned.

Thanks once again to the good folks at Hancock House, without whose skills this whole project would still be a pipe dream in the somewhat fuzzy minds of a couple of backwoods B.S.ers and one great artist. Thanks also to Ginette, Linda and Mark for putting up with us for so long. We know it ain't bin easy!

Call Me a Fool

Mike Puhallo

Call me a fool if you want to
I'll not deny your claim,
for I've spent my life chasin' after
many a foolish game.

I haven't lived my life safely,
I've always played on the edge,
a fool who thinks dreams are a challenge,
and a bet's not a bet if you hedge.

A cowboy, a poet, a dreamer,
a rancher and rodeo hand.
And no great wealth I've acquired,
for money slips through my fingers like sand.

But, I've gathered a treasure of memories,
and the love of a woman that's true.
And these are the things that matter to me
far more than your gold does to you.

And when our journey is over
and the final tally is done,
I know I'll only leave with my memories,
But can you do any better ol' son?

Oh you can call me a fool if you want to,
But boys, I'm proud to report,
I've chased every dream that called me
Cause life ain't a spectator sport!

Of Leather, Hemp and Wood

Brian Brannon

When I sit some nights, all by myself,
    and think of days gone by
I wonder if the things I know
    will pass the day I die.

For packin' is a trade of old,
    a quaint and woodsy lore.
Fast goin' the way of honest men
    not needed any more.

Likewise gone the land we rode
    where needed trees were felled.
A shining wondrous gift of God,
    which few but us beheld.

We carried the freight of a nation's birth
    on the backs of ponies and mules.
Threw the hoolihan, basket and diamond hitch
    had a "sometimes" relation with rules.

Yeah, packers are men like few today,
    a dyin' breed it's said,
Who wear our pants from the inside out,
    to the mountains we are wed.

We'd know the boss-hoss in the string
    from an hour spent on the rails.
We'd know who'd stray, and who'd pack eggs,
    whose head fit to whose tail.

We balanced panniers, without a scale—
    fitted saddles like they should.
Brought our horses to camp with nary a sore,
    made loads ride like they could.

We carried the map of a thousand trails
    tucked there, up under our hats.
And those we'd forgot, our saddle horse knew
    'cause we chose 'em partly for that.

Longshoremen of the equestrian world,
    blue-collared folk it's true.
But I never did mind, 'cause I always could find
    myself in that high mountain blue.

Reg Kesler's Hat

Mike Puhallo

Saskatoon Rodeo, some twenty years ago,
we drove all night, through a blizzard
of prairie wind and snow.
A gray mare called Quick Silver,
was the bronc that I had drawn.
A tall, good lookin' horse,
but tough to get out on.
Some say her momma was a gator,
from down in Louisian.
And I've never seen a horse so keen
to try to bite a man.

Marlin tried to help me out.
He jumped up to shake her mane
but she raked his belly with her teeth,
and he jumped down again.
Now if you've been around Reg Kesler,
you know he's not a quiet man;
and patience is one virtue,
he sure don't understand.

Ol' Reg jumped on the bucking chute
and doffed his brand new hat,
He slapped that pony across the face
but it was ME, he hollered at.
"Hell sakes, what you waitin' for?
Get in your saddle son!
I got the bitch distracted,
get on an get it done!"

I nodded my head, they turned us loose
and things got kinda busy,
the way that ol' gray mare could buck,
had this man darn near dizzy.

I'm tryin' hard to spur that nag,
and barely gettin' by,
when the sound of laughter reaches me
and I can't think of a reason why!
Well, I never drove a thousand miles
to make a fool of me.
But it seemed the harder I tried to spur
the more they giggled with glee!

At last, as a fog bank dissipates
when morning turns to day,
clarity returned and she bucked,
high, and straight away.
And as I charged the front,
I finally saw what folks was laughin' at,
for flopping around from that horse's mouth
was Reg's brand new hat!
Good thing the whistle blew right then,
'cause I plumb lost control
caught up in the spirit of mirth,
as on the ground I roll.
I lay there gigglin' in the dirt,
so overcome with glee,
I hardly noticed the pick up horse
that ran right over me.

Well Reg's two-hundred-dollar hat
was plumb destroyed that day,
But I come up with a "seventy-one"
and a split of fourth-place pay.
And at the same time Reg Kesler,
earned this cowboy's undyin' respect.
For this sacrifice to help a rookie kid
win an eighteen-dollar check!

Shovel Pass

Brian Brannon

You figure you've done some ridin', he says
    well, try this one on for size.
That cavey of ours goes to sleep each night
    up there where that eagle flies.

We was standin' that evenin' 'round base camp
    up high into Shovel Pass,
Southeast of a town called Jasper
    where only the sidehills hold grass.

Them horses'd just naturally wandered
    further up for each blade of grass,
'Til with glasses we just barely saw 'em
    from that camp in the Shovel Pass.

Try it, he says, in the mist of the mornin'
    with only a bridle to hand.
Chase that string down at a lope and a gallop
    and see if you're that kind of man.

Well, back then, I was rawhide and willful
    and maybe some cards short a deck.
So I took up his dare, and said I'd be there
    with no fear of a genuine wreck.

Next mornin' near dawn, the clouds had sat down
    and the dew on the brush mixed with rain,
We set out in slippery, rubber rain pants
    and I started to think once again.

But the deal had been made, and the cards had been drawn
    and no cowboy will take back his word.
So we climbed through the trees, sometimes on our knees
    in search of that high-feedin' herd.

We found 'em up there, where the wind blows the hair

of the goats that'll sometimes be seen.
We caught up our rides, both for shortness and stride,
  headed down for our bacon and beans.

Now, I can't say of course, if you've ever pushed horses
  two men on a thirty-nag string,
But some older ones say, that they ain't seen the day
  that would be a remarkable thing.

Yet you horsemen will know, that once on the go
  that to hold 'em, you've gotta move fast.
If you give 'em the time, they'll turn on a dime
  every which way, 'fore moments are past.

And I often do wonder, if the older ones ponder
  on the slope of that ride that we had
Or the grip our legs lacked, on those slimy, wet backs
  Against rosin, that rubber's sure sad.

No, I can't rightly say, what happened those days
   'cause it all went by in a blur.
I remember wet trees, and a horse 'tween my knees
   and an instant that somehow seemed pure.

And I seem to recall, what was danged near a fall
   with my body wrapped tight 'round a neck,
Of pushin' back in, on a passin' tree limb
   and avoidin' a dangerous wreck.

All that I know, is that rain turned to snow
   and them ponies turned up where they should.
We weathered the ride, never lost any hide,
   what luck that we had, it was good.

Yeah, I think back to then, when my profile was thin,
   'bout those days way back in my past.
And I'm thankful to see, that I ever could be
   ridin' high in the Shovel Pass.

The Stirrup

Brian Brannon

Now, Bax has got him this story
'bout a spur that he found one day
Whilst ridin' the low-water crossin'
chasin' down a few strays.

I got me a story similar,
one item, found all by itself,
Behind the bar in a ghost-town
sittin' up there on a shelf.

And being a horseman, I knew at a glance
that it was a stirrup up there.
It looked to be calvary or RCMP,
might have a story to share.

So I took that old stirrup down into my hand
and knew right away I'd been wrong.
For that stirrup, my friends, had been forged out of bronze
in a time where no cowboy belonged.

No question at all that it came from the east,
it had tigers and dragons embossed,
And I wondered what noble Mandarin family
this obvious heirloom had lost.

For certain I was that it came from North China
and probably a tiny piece further.
Down from the steppes of Mongolia,
where the hordes kept their ponies in lather.

This stirrup had followed one family
out of the mists of time.
And I wondered what favored son of a clan
mighta sold this thing for a dime.

But No! I just can't believe that,
no son of the steppes could have sold
The pride of his father's family,
no matter the price in pure gold.

So, like Bax I'm left with a question
and it's useless to speculate.
How had that stirrup come to B.C.
and what was that family's fate.

I ain't got any answers,
and I'll bet that no horseman will see
the truth of a stirrup, left in a bar
in a ghost-town, in northern B.C.

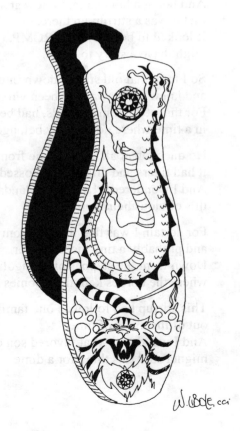

The Stone

Mike Puhallo

A smooth piece of stone
kinda caught my eye
In a shallow river crossing.
It's hard to say why.

Now all river stones are smooth
But this had a different form.
And as stones go in this crossing,
it was larger than the norm.

I swung down from the saddle
and plucked it from the stream.
How long it had laid there waiting
I could only dream...

Was no doubt it was a pestle;
and well, it fit the hand.
A well-used, stone-age food processor
from when this was Indian land.

I thought upon that distant time,
as I handled that piece of stone,
lost in a crossing long ago...
the circumstance unknown.

Perhaps it was lost while fording a flood,
this river can get wild,
or it may have been tossed from a travois pack,
by a careless, playful child.

Such a valuable tool would surely be missed
when the time came to unpack,
unless it was lost in the scramble
to avoid an enemy attack...

Then my pony snorted impatiently,
and I thought I heard a far-off eagle scream,
as I bent down and carefully placed
the stone back in the stream.

N. LIDDLE, cci

Ray Anderson

Brian Brannon

A friend of mine named Ray
   has had a lot to say
In poetry and verse,
   most say he ain't the worse.

He's got some forty published,
   they're in a book you see.
I hope some day to emulate
   he means that much to me.

For he's an old-time cowboy,
   Tom Blasingame up north,
Tyson ain't wrote him in song,
   but that don't negate his worth.

Some say he's rode a thousand storms
   chasin' down young beef.
For you below the forty-ninth
   that's scarce within belief.

Up here things ain't done the same,
   we must consult the weather.
From cuttin' colts, to brandin' calves
   to oilin' down our leather.

But Ray's a man who is above
   the lie of maps and bounds.
He'd rank top cowboy down in hell,
   his equal's hardly found.

Well, cowboy is as cowboy does,
   a dyin' breed we know.
Friend Ray he stands among the best,
   I'm here to tell you so.

Brian
Mike Puhallo

The eyes that have stared down a grizzly
    with just a fishin' pole in hand,
and tracked a wounded wapiti bull
    through a tangled aspen stand.
Now glazed with fear, like a cornered cat,
    glancing furtively about;
surrounded, and trapped, coiled to spring,
    but he can't see any way out.
And the voice that has thundered through canyons
    to keep a six-horse string in line,
Is lost and thinned to a whisper
    like a summer breeze in the pines.
White knuckles gripping the podium,
    he sways for a moment and then,
because the soul of the poet won't weaken,
    he summons his courage again.
He speaks of his life in the mountains
    on horse back, a man among men,
This mountain man, packer and guide,
    who claims the wild critters as kin.
He ponders some, on this strange calling,
    a gift, a blessing or curse,
For he can portray like no other,
    the wild mountains and beasts in his verse.

Tommy

Brian Brannon

A better guide you will not find
    from the Kiabob to Dawson.
He learned the trade at his daddy's knee,
    Art knew the hills and then some.

The two of them, a man and son,
    they rode the Tchaikazuan
Before the rest of us had learned
    to name that awesome land.

They crossed the mighty Spectrum Pass
    on down to Dorothy Lake,
And tarried by Yohettas' shores
    this modern world forsaked.

And then up o'er the Red and White,
    a trail I've yet to find,
They journeyed to Long Meadows' grass
    a taste of heavens' kind.

A short trip down to Lastman
    once past that old graveyard,
Then down the shores of Tuscha
    the home place welcomes, pards.

They built their outfit up from nought
    it's now known wide and far,
From the neon-lights of Nashville town
    to Deutscher hunting bars.

The A-T Bar, it met its end
    one dark and windy day.
Tom found his daddy stiff and cold,
    that's what the stories say.

I met Tom back in eighty-nine,
　　I'm proud to call him friend.
But something had gone out of Tom,
　　I saw it even then.

He'd lost the spark of lovin' life,
　　that joy in livin' free,
Though he'd still the skills he learned those days
　　ridin' at his daddy's knee.

And Tommy's skills, they're finest kind,
　　I'd know his trails in hell.
His hunters think him next to God,
　　can't wait his praise to tell.

But we who know him understand
　　they've known 'bout half what could be,
'Cause since that day he lost his dad
　　Tom's been a keelless ship at sea.

It wasn't only Art that died
　　beside the shores of Tuscha,
We lost two guides that fateful day
　　them's true words, pards—you betcha.

26

The Wild McLeans
Mike Puhallo

He forded the North Thompson by moonlight,
a lone mule deer, fat and sleek,
where his kind had crossed for thousands of years
just down from Heffley Creek.

Then he hears the sound of horses,
and slips into the trees,
four young riders moving fast
with good broncs between their knees.

They splashed across the shallows
and up the eastern side,
and rode right past the thicket
where the buck had chose to hide.

They were headed for the "Seven-O"
to steal old Palmer's pride,
embarked on a bloody trail of infamy,
that began with an evening ride.

Hobby farms and houses,
now line the river's course
and none are left that know the boys
who stole ol' Palmer's horse,

But John Usher is remembered
and the Palmer clan lives on,
and the deer still cross the river
in the ghostly light of dawn.

Tyson

Brian Brannon

You see him at the cuttings
    and you know he don't feel right.
He's the spirit of that coyote
    in the headlights late one night.

He don't fit there at the doings
    or no place where there's a crowd.
Just an out-of-time survivor
    sorta different and too proud.

A conundrum and a paradox
    all wrapped up into one,
The one who fuels the legacy
    for others yet to come.

He rides the way of Blasingame,
    of Russell and Will James,
Those who break the trails in life
    and leave us just their names.

Yeah, some'll say I'm blowin' smoke,
    adrift in whiskey dreams,
I'll tell 'em that the truth in life's
    hardly ever what it seems.

There's some who'll hear Tchaikovsky
    inside a magpie's noise,
The ones who see beginnings
    in the play of girls and boys.

Look around you friends of mine,
    a giant walks with you.
You're seein' history made right now
    just east of downtown Longview.

Peppy San and Jack Drake
Mike Puhallo

Peppy San, now there's a name
    that every horseman knew.
That cuttin' horse from Douglas Lake
    was a champion through and through.
Now his owners and his trainers
    have been recognized enough,
famous horsemen that they are
    with rooms full of trophies and stuff.
But I cowboyed with ol' "Ducky" Drake
    and he was quite a case,
If a spooky cow crashed off through the brush
    He'd let us "kids" give chase.
A cow man with lots of savvy
    He got things done without a fuss.
And he rode drag from the side a bit,
    Claimed ol' "Suzy" didn't like the dust.
He heeled a lot of calves at brandings
    for the one-eleven crews.
But old Jack's real calling
    Was nailin' on horse shoes.
He'd learned that trade in the Cavalry
    back many years ago,
And he'd worked shoeing nags on the race track
    for thirty years or so.
Movie stars and racing greats
    were among his list of friends
But semi-retired in cow camp
    is where my story ends.
So if your tellin' tales of that great horse,
    and none of it is news,
Take a moment to remember
    the cowboy who nailed on his shoes.

Jerry

Brian Brannon

Sinclair is a friend of mine
I'm might proud to claim.
He used to ride the rodeo,
saddle broncin' was his game.

One year he wore THE buckle,
the champion, number one.
He lived the life, he lost a wife,
that rodeo's pure fun.

Since he's met Miss Lana
he's kinda settled down.
Instead of ropin' cows, these days
he's haulin' them around.

That don't mean he's lost the fire
he's still that man and more.
He loves to take a mouthy drunk
and mop the barroom floor.

I met him on a film set
out on the Morley plain.
His boy named Lee, Sinclair and me
we tried the movie game.

We went one night for drinks and fun,
the picture crew was payin'.
I knew right then we'd long be friends,
do you follow what I'm sayin'?

'Cause I'm a man who likes his fun,
can't stand to be constricted.
I'm born a hundred years too late
with modern things conflicted.

In him I sensed a kindred soul

with him I'll ride the river.
Real cowboys are a dyin' breed,
them others can't deliver.

And though we don't keep contact much,
it really isn't needed.
We know we're friends 'til history ends,
the truth of that's conceded.

Humility

Mike Puhallo

No one really walks alone,
    although the truth ain't always clear.
Someone blazed the trail you followed
    and someone brought you here.
And all the gifts and talents,
    with which you might be blessed
are things you could not give yourself
    nor could you, to me, bequest.
So what is there to brag about
    and swell yourself with pride,
for we are but the vessel
    in which the gift may ride.
So hold to your humility
    in simple gratitude each day
thank Him from whom all gifts flow,
    and thank those who've shown the way.

Wild Rags and Silver Hooks

Brian Brannon

I see them western saddles
   with the comfort built right in
And I wonder to myself sometimes
   where's the cowboys that has been?

Where are those guys who rode them kaks
   that was built for workin' folks,
Who wore their pants from the inside out?
   Today's cowboys are jokes.

The kinda guy who rode a horse
   on C. M. Russell's range
Would ride December in summer gear
   and hand the boss some change.

They worked from can until can't see,
   got less than welfare pay.
They stuck the job, they kept their word,
   try'n show me that today.

Now the focus of a lot of folks
   is on cowboys today.
They yearn to leave the cities 'hind
   and taste a bygone day.

And they find it in them charlatans
   who wear a cowboy hat,
Who ride a horse and talk like salts,
   we know the truth of that.

They live in mansions that'd twist the mind
   of an old-time workin' hand.
They got 'spense accounts and taxin' deals
   and invest in Khruger rands.

They count their beef on computer discs,
    spend winters in old Mexico.
They're as close to C. M. Russell's world
    as an outhouse in Jerico.

Let me tell you orphans a story
    'bout some cowboys that's danged-sure for real,
Who pushed a herd past the Itchas,
    ate bannoch and moose for their meals.

They crossed an uncharted country
    in the thirties of Canada's teens.
It was grass to the belly of a curly red cow,
    country no white man had seen.

They was long on courage and bottom
    learned that in the Buffalo State,
They had dreams of a cattleman's empire
    gave their all to the call of their fate.

They were Panhandle Phillips and Hobson
    and they cared not a whit for convention.
They took 'em a chance, and built the Home ranch
    on the strength of their own conviction.

Now, lesser men will criticize
    and find fault where they can,
But, in their hearts, they know the truth
    they ain't but half the man.

So cowboys, ride your padded seats
    wear wild-rags and silver hooks,
And dream of the day you'll be okay
    in Pan and Hobson's books.

Song of the Night Owl

Mike Puhallo

I pity those who fear the night,
doors and windows bolted tight.
The urban folk who flee indoors
and abandon their streets
to the thiefs and whores.
They spend a fortune on street lamps
to hold back the night.
And then never dare
to walk into their light.

Far off down the valley
I see the faint glow,
and pity the fools
who'll never know
the awesome glory of a starlit sky
With a meteor shower in late July,
or to ride across a meadow
beneath an August moon,
serenaded by the midnight song of a loon.

A night owl I am
and always will be,
for the night sky's a vision
that sets my soul free.

Chilcotin Skunk

Mike Puhallo

When Diana walked out to the greenhouse
    good lord how that place stunk.
It seems their Chilcotin veggie patch
    had been visited by a skunk.
She threw wide the door
    to air the place out,
and when her teary eyes could see
    she noticed the striped vermin
had ate all the broccoli!
    When the tale was then relayed to me,
I knew it wasn't bunk
    So I asked my nephew right away,
"How did you train that skunk?"

It's Hard to Finger Them Bears

Brian Brannon

Heinrich and I was huntin' one day,
lookin' for grizzly bears.
We'd filled his moose tag two days ago
and were ridin' along with no cares.

It was gettin' late on into the evenin'
so we'd tarried for a while
On this hill above an old moose kill.
I guess you could call it a rock pile.

We'd glassed just a couple of moments
'til Heinrich'd bellered out,
"Hey! There's a grizzly bear down there
tossin' turf about."

So I brought my glasses up in line
and sure enough I saw
This big, old boar a tossin' sod
on high with both his paws.

And pardners, let me tell you
that bear was raisin' hell,
I figured he'd learn to speak Chinese
before the darkness fell.

Now, grizzlies, they normally bury their grub
to kinda percolate.
It cooks there, 'neath the sod and sun,
all the bear needs do is wait.

So we'd peg Mr. Claws that day at dusk
we'd catch him durin' sunrise.
We would have the sun behind our backs
and hand ole bruin a big surprise.

Come mornin' we was up at five

Heinrich, he was hurtin'.
We'd lose that bear, we'd seen last night
of that he was near certain.

Now, me, I wasn't bothered none
'cause I kinda know them bears.
We'd find our bear upon his kill
though Heinrich did despair.

We was off that morn' into the dark,
left our nags behind.
We'd catch that boar at the crack of dawn
and see what luck we'd find.

We put the wind into our face,
the sun against our back.
We walked up to a hundred yards,
there was nothin' that we lacked.

Ole bear, he stood upon that kill
and challenged all he found.
We carried a pump, and a seven mag
Against lightnin' times nine hundred pounds.

Now, one thing you should know, old pards,
that seven was sighted at three.
But Heinrich and I'd forgot them stats
while he'd sighted against that tree.

The gun was dead on at three hundred yards,
but at that place, that day, where we stood
The bullet that Heinrich let fly in the dawn
hit four inches higher than it should.

The boar, he tumbled off the kill
then bounded up like a shot.
He headed down our line of sight
let me tell you, he was hot.

Heinrich, he threw up his seven mag
and squeezed the trigger quick.
I looked to see a brown mountain fall
and all I heard was click.

I pushed ole Heinrich to the side,
brought my back-up up in line,
I figured eight shots from that pump
might change ole grizzly's mind.

But pardners, Murphy's Law was showin'
there'd be nothin' I'd be hittin'.
I pulled the trigger twice, good folks,
and then I started shittin'.

W. LIDDLE. cci

'Cause that bear, he had me by the shoulder
and his teeth, they sank right in.
I wondered what in hell to do
as he tossed me out my skin.

Well I got to thinkin' right desperate
and if you think I'm kiddin' you,
Just picture yourselves in a grizzly bear's jaws
and tell me what you'd do.

Me, I reached down casually
stuck my finger up his butt.
And if you think you've got a better idea
why, I wish you lots of luck.

Ole Bear, he really was shocked my friends
and he jumped off with standin' hair,
Had both of his butt-cheeks tightly clamped
took off this finger, right there.

Now, most folks'll say that they know danged near certain
that a grizzly's got teeth in the front of 'im.
But few know the truth, that the bear has in fact
some others hid down in the back of him.

So that is exactly how I lost this one finger
up north where the sun shines forever.
I stuck it, old pards, in a hole where it seems
that the sun seems to shine hardly never.

Herd Instinct

Mike Puhallo

Them politicians run in herds,
  much as cattle do.
And to my way of thinkin',
  the cow's the brighter of the two!
For she supports the rancher
  who provides her feed and hay,
and rarely bites the hand that feeds her,
  for that's not the bovine way.
But us farmers, and us ranchers
  also feed them urban herds,
and they return the favor,
  with silly laws and fightin' words.
And while a cow herd sometimes panics
  and gallops off with speed,
There's nothing quite as mindless
  as a political stampede!

Groomin' Gizmos

Brian Brannon

I seen this advertisement in
   a magazine one day
About this vacuum cleaner that would
   groom your horse they say.

Now I don't know how your horses are
   or how in hell they're trained,
You try that on the ones we ride
   you'll danged sure get you maimed.

Our horses ain't real flighty folks,
   they're just the common breed.
These modern groom contraptions though
   are more than what they need.

I guess we never saw the cause
   to doll 'em up like some.
For nags aworkin' in the hills
   that stuff seems kinda dumb.

And dumb you'd be, I'll tell ya friends
   to try that on Qaddaffi.
He's a painted pack horse folks,
   his sense of humor's iffy.

He'd probably see and hear that thing
   and guess you was some bear.
He'd stomp your boodie in the dust
   and leave you lyin' there.

So genteel folk, you keep them jokes,
   your pampered darlin's blow-dry.
The day we need their like out here,
   I'll get me down to hell and fry.

Ode to Round Bales

Mike Puhallo

Sunrise up on Bambric Creek,
    Coast mountains all aglow,
and just a wee bit chilly
    at forty-five below.
When the wind blows
    from the coast range,

cold as a banker's heart,
    the cows are kinda gaunt
and the tractor just won't start.
    As you work to make the damn thing run,
all through the frozen day,
    You kinda wish you'd stuck to loose stacks,
a well-broke team and sleigh.

The Long and the Short of It

Mike Puhallo

I've known me some long-winded cowboys,
and while they can be entertainin' at times
I've noticed that the best of the workin' kind
usually stick to the shortest of rhymes!

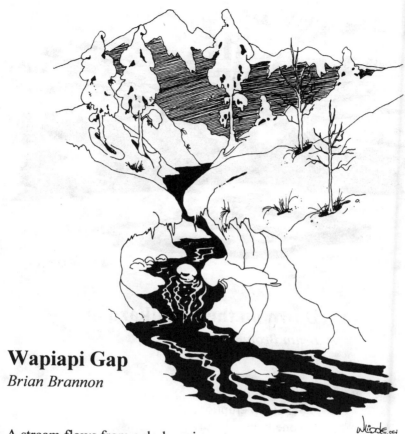

Wapiapi Gap
Brian Brannon

A stream flows from a dark ravine
    On a shoulder nearby,
Aspens creak and pines whisper.

On a frosty night
    Moonlight lays a scintillating carpet of diamonds
On a blanket of deep powdery snow
    That somehow, gives the impression of warmth.

In every direction you look,
    Clarity gains new meaning—
Hauntingly.

N.LIDDLE, cci

Dawn on the Tchaikazuan
Brian Brannon

Flowing union
   or sharp eruption,
No one knows I fear.

Pregnant stillness,
   more than silence,
Nature changing gears.

Muted velvet
   fleeing westward,
A crystal carpet stays.

Glorious, golden
   sunrise follows,
Announcing newborn day.

East or West

Mike Puhallo

Well-manicured white paddocks,
    no weeds or burrs around.
Well-groomed equine aristocrats
    who's range is an acre of ground.
I suppose its kinda pretty,
    this orderly equine world,
where flat saddles are the rule
    and no lariats are twirled.
But boys, if I was a horse
    it ain't too hard to see
I'd rather join the wild bunch,
    in the sageland runnin' free.

Wolves

Mike Puhallo

There's a whole lot of town dogs,
that dream wolfish dreams,
and crave to howl at the moon.
But they best stick to the porch
and stay out of the sage
when they try to mimic our tunes.

Our hairs kinda scruffy,
and matted with burrs.
We're rain-soaked, foul-smelling,
despicable curs.
Such is often the appearance
of the true western child.
Born on the range and raised in the wild.

We don't take much care in our groomin' it's true,
for in Northern wolf packs, four legged or two,
each cur's only rated
by the things he can do.

And any sheep, in wolf's clothing
would damn soon show up.
'Cause when you run with the dogs,
you don't squat like a pup.

And all those lap dogs
that just have to howl
Best stay close to the porch
'Cause the wolf's on the prowl.

W. LIDDLE, cci

The Tchaikazuan

Brian Brannon

Tchaikazuan, spirit land,
   I've tried so very long
To find the words to write of you,
   I'm somehow always wrong.

Why can't I sing in praise of you,
   your beauty so sublime.
It seems so very strange to me,
   I am your living shrine.

My mind is filled with many words
   like rugged, savage, grandeur,
Mysterious, awesome, majesty,
   pristine alpine splendor.

And though these words do fill my soul,
   they'll not to paper come
In such a way, to homage pay
   their representing sum.

Then a thought struck through my mind,
   brushed jumbled words aside.
I cannot tell a soul of you,
   they must with you abide.

For can a lover tell the world
   how sweet beloved lips
or can a sailor share his joy
   astride the deck of ships?

So I must bear forever more
    inside the heart of me
The awe and wonder that I feel
    when'er I think of thee.

And as for them that's never been
    wrapped in your valley's arms,
They'll never know, until they go,
    the magic of your charms.

Home

Mike Puhallo

They subdivided the homestead,
while I was off at school
Pop kept enough for a hobby farm,
two horses and a mule.

So I was a horse man left afoot,
a cowboy with no cattle,
who'd rather ride colts in a round corral,
than hear that chute gate rattle.

Lost out on the rodeo trail,
or drivin' truck for wages,
Tryin' to build a stake for a ranch of my own,
an' boys its takin' me ages.

Well I finally got my ranch,
a mortgage with the bank to boot.
So I'm bustin' my ass to pay for the place
as trapped as a bronc in the chute.

Sometimes, for the life of me,
I can't quite decide
If the vision at the end of the trail
was really worth the ride.

But, there's a girl who's journeyed beside me,
near every step of the way,
since she gathered me up at a rodeo dance,
a lost and ornery stray.

She brought to my life some sanity,
that I could never find on my own
and any place she'd stand beside me,
would soon become a home.

And I suppose that's what I was hunting for
through all those lonely miles
a chance to feel like I belonged
in a world of tests and trials.

Now my little ranch ain't so much,
a few acres of pasture and field,
but my Linda's love makes it home
and this cowboy's fate is sealed.

Cowboy Confusion

Mike Puhallo

How come they call it common sense
    when it's so rare and hard to find?
And the harder I try to get ahead
    the further I fall behind.
Some claim I'm worth a bundle,
    with land and cattle all round,
But my pockets used to have more jingle
    on cowboy wages and found.

Chores

Mike Puhallo

The fact that a good man's hard to find,
    can make my wife kinda miserable.
'cause whenever she's got chores for me,
    I get plumb invisible!

Carpe Diems

Mike Puhallo

Whether you travel the high and rocky trail
    or the low road, smooth and wide,
No destination is assured,
    so you'd best enjoy the ride.

MORE GREAT HANCOCK HOUSE TITLES

History

Barkerville
Lorraine Harris
ISBN 0-88839-152-8

B.C.'s Own Railroad
Lorraine Harris
ISBN 0-88839-125-0

Cariboo Gold Rush Story
Donald Waite
ISBN 0-88839-202-8

The Craigmont Story
Murphy Shewchuk
ISBN 0-88839-980-4

Curse of Gold
Elizabeth Hawkins
ISBN 0-88839-281-8

Early History of Port Moody
Dorothea M. Norton
ISBN 0-88839-197-8

End of Custer
Dale T. Schoenberger
ISBN 0-88839-288-5

Fishing in B.C.
Forester & Forester
ISBN 0-919654-43-6

Fraser Canyon Highway
Lorraine Harris
ISBN 0-88839-182-X

Fraser Canyon Story
Donald E. Waite
ISBN 0-88839-204-4

Fraser Valley Story
Donald E. Waite
ISBN 0-88839-203-6

Gold Creeks & Ghost Towns
N. L. (Bill) Barlee
ISBN 0-88839-988-X

Gold! Gold!
Joseph Petralia
ISBN 0-88839-118-8

Living with Logs
Donovan Clemson
ISBN 0-919654-44-4

Lost Mines & Historic Treasures
N. L. (Bill) Barlee
ISBN 0-88839-992-8

The Mackenzie Yesterday
Alfred P. Aquilina
ISBN 0-88839-083-1

Pioneering Aviation of the West
Lloyd M. Bungey
ISBN 0-88839-271-0

Vancouver Recalled
Derek Pethick
ISBN 0-919654-09-6

Yukon Places & Names
R. Coutts
ISBN 0-88826-082-2